To

From

Written and compiled by by Lois Rock
Illustrations copyright © 2015 Kay Widdowson
This edition copyright © 2015 Lion Hudson

Published by Lion Children's Books
an imprint of

Lion Hudson plc

Wilkinson House, Jordan Hill Road,
Oxford OX2 8DR, England
www.lionhudson.com/lionchildrens

ISBN 978 0 7459 6552 9

First edition 2015

Acknowledgments

All unattributed prayers are by Lois Rock, copyright © Lion Hudson.

p. 8: Sarah Betts Rhodes (1829–1904)

p. 18: From an old New England sampler

p. 28: Cecil Frances Alexander (1818–95)

p. 32: Victoria Tebbs, copyright © Lion Hudson

p. 35: Edith Rutter Leatham (1870–1939)

p. 48b: Julia Carney (1823–1908)

p. 58: John Leland (1754–1841)

p. 59: Christina Goodings, copyright © Lion Hudson

Bible extracts are taken or adapted from the Good News Bible © 1994 published by the Bible Societies/HarperCollins Publishers Ltd UK, Good News Bible© American Bible Society 1966, 1971, 1976, 1992. Used with permission.

The Lord's Prayer (p. 55) as it appears in *Common Worship: Services and Prayers for the Church of England* (Church House Publishing, 2000) is copyright © The English Language Liturgical Consultation and is reproduced by permission of the publisher.

A catalogue record for this book is available from the British Library

Printed and bound in China, January 2015, LH17

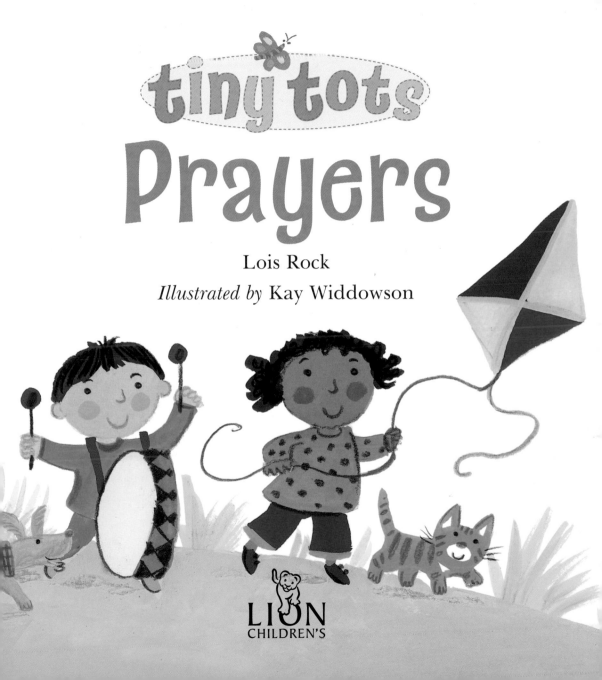

tiny tots
Prayers

Lois Rock

Illustrated by Kay Widdowson

LION
CHILDREN'S

Contents

Hello God 6

Can you see me, God?   8

Can you hear me, God?   10

My counting prayer   12

Helping hands   16

God Bless Us All   18

God bless my family   20

Thank you for my home   22

Thank you for my food   24

Thank you for kind people   26

God's Wonderful World   28

Thank you for the day   30

Whatever the weather   32

We share this world   34

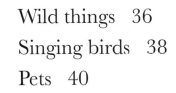

Wild things   36

Singing birds   38

Pets   40

A Child of God   42

God is love   44

Singing praises   46

Following Jesus   48

Saying sorry   50

The good shepherd   52

The prayer Jesus gave   54

Now the Day is Over   56

An angel to watch over me   58

Goodnight   60

Index of First Lines   62

My star prayer   64

Hello God

God, look down from heaven:
Here on earth you'll see
Someone looking upwards –
That someone is me.

Can you see me, God?

God, who made the earth,
The air, the sky, the sea,
Who gave the light its birth,
Careth for me.

Children's hymn, 19th century

God has counted the stars in the heavens,
God has counted the leaves on the tree;
God has counted the children on earth:
I know God has counted me.

Can you hear me, God?

Here I am, God,
Crouching small.

Here I am, God,
Standing tall.

Now I'm jumping
Like a clown.

Now I'm still
And sitting down.

Now I'm praying:
Can you hear?

If you can, dear God,
Come near.

11

My counting prayer

This is my prayer number 1:
Bless the day that's just begun.

This is my prayer number 2:
May the sky be clear and blue.

This is my prayer number 3:
God, please take good care of me.

This is my prayer number 4:
Help me love you more and more.

This is my prayer number 5:
Make me glad to be alive.

This is my prayer number 6:
Help me when I'm in a fix.

This is my prayer number 7:
Make this world a bit like heaven.

This is my prayer number 8:
Put an end to hurt and hate.

This is my prayer number 9:
Let the light of kindness shine.

This is my prayer number 10:
Bring me safe to bed again.

Helping hands

May my hands be helping hands
 For all that must be done
 That fetch and carry, lift and hold
And make the hard jobs fun.

May my hands be clever hands
In all I make and do
With sand and dough and clay and things
With paper, paint and glue.

May my hands be gentle hands
And may I never dare
To poke and prod nor hurt and harm
But touch with love and care.

God Bless Us All

God bless all those that I love;
God bless all those that love me;
God bless all those that love those that I love,
And all those that love those that love me.

19

God bless my family

Dear God, bless all my family,
as I tell you each name;
and please bless each one differently
for no one's quite the same.

God bless us all
through the bright blue day.
God bless us all
through the dark grey night.
God bless us all
when we hug together.
God bless us all
when we're out of sight.

21

Thank you for my home

Bless the window
Bless the door
Bless the ceiling
Bless the floor
Bless this place which is our home
Bless us as we go and come.

22

Thank you for my food

Let us take a moment
To thank God for our food,
For friends around the table
And everything that's good.

For health and strength
and daily food,
we praise your name,
O Lord.

Traditional

Thank you for kind people

Thank you, dear God,
for the many kind people
who help us along on our way,
who smile when we laugh
and who care when we cry
and who keep us safe all through the day.

God's Wonderful World

All things bright and beautiful,
All creatures great and small,
All things wise and wonderful,
The Lord God made them all.

Children's hymn, 19th century

Thank you for the day

Thank you, God in heaven,
For a day begun.
Thank you for the breezes,
Thank you for the sun.
For this time of gladness,
For our work and play,
Thank you, God in heaven,
For another day.

Traditional

31

Whatever the weather

The sun may shine
The rain may fall
God will always
Love us all.

Victoria Tebbs

God of Noah
God of flood
God of puddles
God of mud
God of rainbows
God of sky
Turn the weather
Round to dry.

33

We share this world

Baby creatures, just awakened,
You are part of God's creation;
Baby creatures, oh, so small,
God is father of us all.

Dear Father, hear and bless
your beasts and singing birds;
and guard with tenderness
small things that have no words.

Children's prayer, 20th century

35

Wild things

Bless the hungry lion
and its ROAR

Bless the big brown bear
that likes to GROWL

36

Bless the sly hyena and its scary HA HA HA

Bless the wolves who see the moon and HOWL.

Singing birds

God bless the birds of springtime
that twitter in the trees
and flutter in the hedgerows
and soar upon the breeze.

God bless the birds of summer
that gather on the shore
and glide above the ocean
where breakers crash and roar.

God bless the birds of autumn
as they prepare to fly
and fill the damp and chilly air
with wild and haunting cry.

God bless the birds of winter
that hop across the snow
and peck the fallen seeds and fruits
of summer long ago.

Pets

Dear God,
May our dog be loyal and obedient
and patient and gentle and kind
and fun. May everyone in the
family learn to be like that too.

Dear God,
Please bless the cat.
Make it wild enough to be a great explorer.
Make it tame enough to come back home.

A Child of God

I will choose the narrow path,
I will walk the straight,
Through the wide and winding world
Up to heaven's gate.

Based on Matthew 7:13–14

God is love

Praise him, praise him,
All ye little children,
God is love, God is love;
Praise him, praise him,
All ye little children,
God is love, God is love.

Love him…

Thank him…

Children's hymn, anonymous

44

Love is giving, not taking,
mending, not breaking,
trusting, believing,
never deceiving,
patiently bearing
and faithfully sharing
each joy, every sorrow,
today and tomorrow.

Anonymous

45

Singing praises

Praise God on the noisy drum
Rumpty tumpty tumpty tum.

Praise God with a mighty clash
Make the cymbals crash-a-bash.

Praise God on the gentle flute
Tootle tootle tootle toot.

Praise God as you pluck the strings
Tring a ling a ling a ling.

Play the trumpet, rum pah pah
May your praises sound afar.

From Psalm 150

Following Jesus

I'm learning to be more like Jesus,
I'm learning the right way to live.
I'm learning to show loving kindness,
I'm learning to truly forgive.

Little deeds of kindness,
Little words of love,
Help to make earth happy,
Like the heaven above.

Children's hymn, 19th century

Saying sorry

I told God everything:
I told God about all the bad things I had done.
I gave up trying to pretend.
I gave up trying to hide.
I knew that the only way was to own up
 and say sorry.
And God forgave me.

From Psalm 32:5

Dear God,
I am your lost sheep.
Please come and find me.
Please take me home.

From Luke 15:1–7

The good shepherd

Dear God, you are my shepherd,
You give me all I need,
You take me where the grass grows green
And I can safely feed.

You take me where the water
Is quiet and cool and clear;
And there I rest and know I'm safe
For you are always near.

From Psalm 23

The prayer Jesus gave

"When you pray," said Jesus, "do not use a lot of words. Your Father God already knows what you need before you ask him.

"This, then, is what you should pray:

"Our Father in heaven,
hallowed be your name,
your kingdom come,
your will be done,
on earth as in heaven.
Give us today our daily bread.
Forgive us our sins
as we forgive those who sin against us.
Lead us not into temptation
but deliver us from evil."

From Matthew 6 and Luke 11

Now the Day is Over

Day is done,
Gone the sun
From the lake,
From the hills,
From the sky.
Safely rest,
All is well!
God is nigh.

Anonymous

56

57

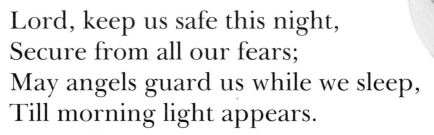

An angel to watch over me

Lord, keep us safe this night,
Secure from all our fears;
May angels guard us while we sleep,
Till morning light appears.

Children's prayer, 18th century

58

Clouds in the sky above,
Waves on the sea,
Angels up in heaven
Watching over you and me.

Christina Goodings

59

Goodnight

Now I lay me down to sleep,
I pray thee, Lord, thy child to keep;
Thy love to guard me through the night
And wake me in the morning light.

Traditional

When I lie down, I go to sleep in peace;
you alone, O Lord, keep me perfectly safe.

Psalm 4:8

Index of First Lines

A

All things bright and beautiful   28

B

Baby creatures, just awakened   34

Bless the hungry lion and its ROAR
   36

Bless the window   22

C

Clouds in the sky above   59

D

Day is done   56

Dear Father, hear and bless   35

Dear God, Please bless the cat   41

Dear God, bless all my family   20

Dear God, I am your lost sheep   51

Dear God, May our dog be loyal
   and obedient   40

Dear God, you are my shepherd
   52

F

For health and strength   24

G

God bless all those that I love   18

God bless the birds of springtime
   38

God bless us all through the bright
   blue day   21

God has counted the stars in the
   heavens   9

God of Noah   33

God, look down from heaven   6

God, who made the earth   8

H

Here I am, God   10

I

I told God everything   50

I will choose the narrow path   42

I'm learning to be more like Jesus   48

L

Let us take a moment   24
Little deeds of kindness   48
Lord, keep us safe this night   58
Love is giving, not taking   45

M

May my hands be helping hands   16
May my life shine   64

N

Now I lay me down to sleep   60

P

Praise God on the noisy drum   46
Praise him, praise him, All ye little children   44

T

Thank you, dear God, for the many kind people   26
Thank you, God in heaven, For a day begun   30
The sun may shine   32
This is my prayer number 1   12

W

When I lie down, I go to sleep in peace   60
"When you pray," said Jesus, "do not use a lot of words"   54

My star prayer

May my life shine
Like a star in the night,
Filling my world
With goodness and light.

From Philippians 2:15